1·2·3 Rhymes, Stories & Songs

Open-Ended Language Experiences For Young Children

Formerly published as *Story Time*

By Jean Warren

Illustrated by Marion Hopping Ekberg

Totline PUBLICATIONS

Warren Publishing House
A Division of Frank Schaffer Publications
Torrance, California

Editorial Staff:

Gayle Bittinger, Kathleen Cubley, Brenda Lalonde

Production Staff:

Eileen Carbary, Jill Lustig

Computer Graphics:

Kathy Kotomaimoce, Eric Stovall

ISBN 0-911019-50-2

Library of Congress Catalog Card Number 91-67075
Printed in the United States of America
Published by: Warren Publishing House

Editorial Office: P.O. Box 2250
            Everett, WA 98203
Business Office: 23740 Hawthorne Blvd.
            Torrance, CA 90505

20 19 18 17 16 15 14 13 12 11 10 9 8 7 6

Contents

Introduction

Young children need many kinds of language experiences. They need open-ended language activities that can help them solve problems and create new ideas as much as they need structured activities to learn correct usage and pronunciation.

1-2-3 Rhymes, Stories and Songs gives teachers and parents creative opportunities that can turn a young child's everyday experiences into rich language experiences. While the lead-in text for each activity does not limit the content or the length of the children's responses, it is written in such a way as to encourage the children to develop their own ideas as they follow along. The responses children make in this book are guided by the theme and a natural story progression.

The activities in this book can be used with many children in a circle or with just one child on your lap. Children can participate differently according to their ages and abilities. Encouraging and accepting as "correct" all responses, even the absurd ones, helps to foster your children's self-esteem. Children should feel free to contribute without worrying about limitations or consequences. In this unconditional atmosphere, they will experience immediate success and have the confidence to be creative and open in their answers.

I am always delighted when I present these language activities to a group of young children. Their enthusiasm is contagious. I know you will also love them and want to repeat them often with your children.

Jean Warren

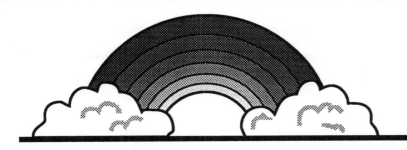

The Trunk

While searching for treasures the other day

I found a big trunk packed far away.

I opened the trunk, and what did I find?

Wonderful treasures of every kind.

On top of the pile was a great big _____.

Then I discovered two old _____.

Next was a shiny black _____.

My favorite was a _____.

The most beautiful treasure was a _____.

The bottom of the trunk was filled with _____.

Trick-Or-Treaters

Knock, knock, sounds like more

Trick-or-treaters at my door.

I open the door and what do I see?

Two green _____ smiling at me.

Knock, knock, sounds like more

Trick-or-treaters at my door.

I open the door and what do I see?

A great big _____ smiling at me.

Knock, knock, sounds like more

Trick-or-treaters at my door.

I open the door and what do I see?

A tiny, tiny _____ smiling at me.

Other possible endings:

An ugly old _____ smiling at me.
A funny brown _____ smiling at me.
Three orange _____ smiling at me.
A big white _____ smiling at me.
Ten little _____ smiling at me.

Vegetable Man

While I was walking down the street,

A vegetable man, I happened to meet.

His head was a bumpy _____.

His arms were long _____.

His body was a large _____.

His legs were two green _____.

His feet were round _____.

His fingers and toes were red _____.

He looked so good that on a hunch

I invited the man home for lunch!

Sunshine

The morning sun peeked through the trees
To kiss the _____ and the honey bees.
It danced by the _____ and the field of hay.
Until it reached the _____ where it stayed all day.

Sun, sun don't you run
Stay with me and have some fun.
Shine on the _____, shine on me.
Shine on the _____, shine on the tree.
Shine on the _____, shine so fair
Shine on the _____, shine everywhere!

Old Bombay

Ready, set, go! We're on our way,
Off to visit old Bombay.

First we'll ride on a _____ going our way,
As we travel to old Bombay.

Next we'll catch a _____ going our way,
On our journey to old Bombay.

Then we'll hop aboard a _____ going our way,
As we travel to old Bombay.

At last we'll jump on a _____ going our way,
On our journey to old Bombay.

Here we are at last in old Bombay,
Traveling can be fun if you know your way!

Bumble

I have a dog named Bumble
Who lives at home with me.
Sometimes he likes to hide
Then my dog I cannot see.

I looked in the _____.
I looked over the _____.
I looked behind the _____.
I looked under the _____.
Now where can BUMBLE BE?

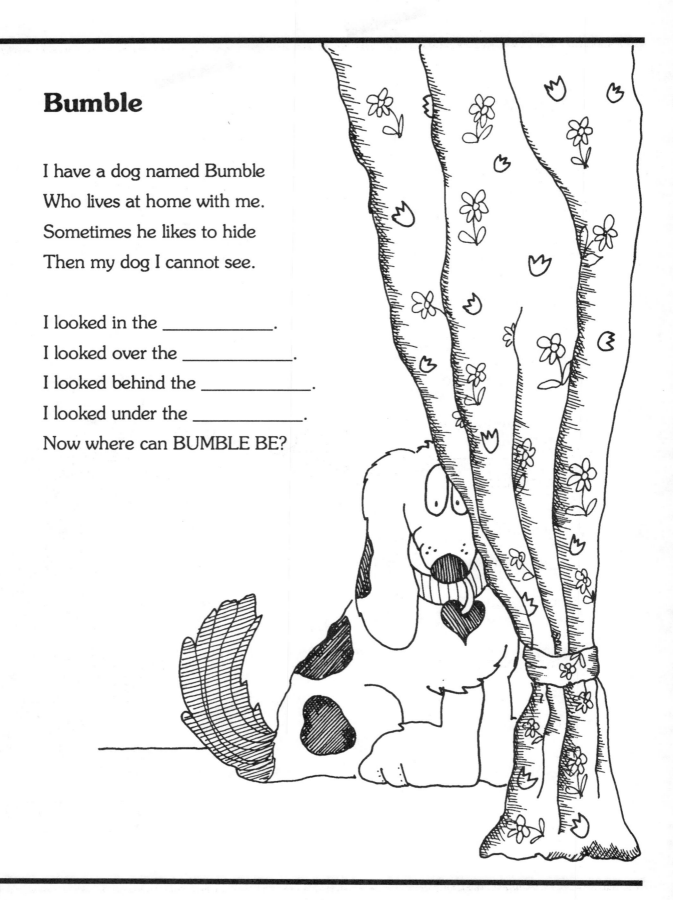

Waiter, Waiter

Waiter, waiter, on the run,
I love _____,
Bring me one.

Waiter, waiter, dressed in blue,
I love _____,
Bring me two.

Waiter, waiter, by the tree,
I love _____,
Bring me three.

Waiter, waiter, by the door,
I love _____,
Bring me four.

Waiter, waiter, sakes alive,
I love _____,
Bring me five.

Jumping Jack

Poor, poor Jumping Jack
He jumped so far he never came back.
He jumped over _____.
And he jumped over _____.
He jumped over _____.
And he never came back.

What I Found

I found a _____

And what do you know?

My little _____ started to grow.

I found a _____

And what do you think?

My little _____ started to shrink.

I found a _____

And what do you say?

My little _____ ran away.

When I Sing

When I sing like a _____
My voice is so high.
When I sing like a _____
My arms want to fly.

When I sing like a _____
My voice is down low.
When I sing like a _____
I touch my big toe.

When I Dance

When I dance like a _____
I turn around.
When I dance like a _____
I touch the ground.

When I twirl like a _____
My hands go up high.
When I twirl like a _____
I reach to the sky.

When I leap like a _____
I wear a frown.
When I leap like a _____
I always fall down.

What Did I See?

I looked outside and what did I see?

A beautiful _____ smiling at me.

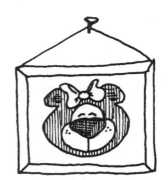

I looked up high and what did I see?

A colorful _____ smiling at me.

I looked in the box and what did I see?

A tiny, tiny _____ smiling at me.

Three Little Froggies

Three little froggies went down to the pond
Down to the pond to play.
Along came a giant _____
And chased one froggie away!

Two little froggies went down to the pond
Down to the pond to play.
Along came a purple _____
And chased one froggie away!

One little froggie went down to the pond
Down to the pond to play.
Along came a flying _____
And chased that froggie away!

Now no little froggies went down to the pond
Down to the pond to play.
Where do you think the froggies went
When they all hopped away?

Little Owl

Little owl, little owl, sitting up high.

Little owl, little owl, what do you spy?

I spy a green _____ out tonight.

I spy a green _____, what a sight!

Little owl, little owl, sitting up high.

Little owl, little owl, what do you spy?

I spy an orange _____ out tonight,

I spy an orange _____, what a sight!

Little owl, little owl, sitting up high.

Little owl, little owl, what do you spy?

I spy a white _____ out tonight.

I spy a white _____, what a sight!

Little owl, little owl, sitting up high.

Little owl, little owl, what do you spy?

I spy a black _____ out tonight.

I spy a black _____, what a sight!

Stop and Shop

I'm going shopping.

My first stop's a _____ shop.

What will I buy today?

A _____ for me,

A _____ for Mother,

A _____ for Sister and

A _____ for Brother.

That's what I'll buy today.

My second stop's a _____ shop.

What will I buy today?

A _____ for me,

A _____ for Mother,

A _____ for Sister and

A _____ for Brother

That's what I'll buy today.

Have the children take turns naming shops and the things they would buy at each one.

Birthday Cake

Baker, baker will you make

A great big _____ birthday cake?

_____ cake,

Make, make, make!

_____ cake,

Bake, bake, bake!

Make, make, make! Bake, bake, bake!

Here's your _____ birthday cake.

Have one child name a kind of cake to make in the first verse. Have the rest of the children recite the remaining verses as they pretend to be bakers and make the cake.

Strange Little Animal

As I was walking down the street.

A strange little animal I happened to meet.

He had a long _____.

And two big _____.

His fur was all _____.

And he walked like a _____.

He liked to eat _____.

On the top of his head was a _____.

He looked so silly, so different and new

I knew right away, he belonged at the zoo!

The Parade

Here comes the parade
Marching down the street.
Everyone is waving
At everyone they meet.

First come the _____
Keeping in a line.
Next come the _____
Looking really fine.

On top of the elephant
A little _____ rides.
Then I see the _____
Coming down both sides.

The _____ are exciting
I love them like the rest.
But if you really want to know
I love the _____ best.

Choosing a Pie

I went to the bakery

To buy a pie,

Which one to choose?

Oh me, oh my!

The biggest was a _____ pie.

The sweetest was a _____ pie.

The tallest was a _____ pie.

The juiciest was a _____ pie.

The smallest was a _____ pie.

Home from the bakery with my pie

Can't wait 'til dinner,

And you know why!

As I Went Walking

As I went walking down the street.

A giant _____ I happened to meet.

He looked so lonely, so very sad

I took him home, which made him glad.

I hid him in _____ during the day.

Then let him out at night, to romp and play.

I couldn't keep my secret for long

For the giant _____ was ever so strong.

He pushed down the door and started to roam

Upstairs and downstairs in our home.

He broke all the _____.

He stepped on the _____.

He sat on the _____.

He rolled over the _____.

He squashed the _____.

My mother came running, my dad came too.

And before you knew it, the _____ was in the zoo!

So if you're out walking down the street.

And if a giant _____ you happen to meet.

Think twice before taking that _____ home.

'Cause you never know where he'll decide to roam!

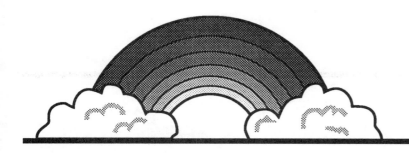

SONGS

Smells Like Dinner

Sung to: "Frere Jacques"

Smells like dinner,

Smells like dinner.

Mmmm, mmmm good.

Mmmm, mmmm good.

I can smell the _____,

I can smell the _____.

Mmmm, mmmm good.

Mmmm, mmmm good.

Have the children take turns naming their favorite
dinner smells to sing about. Repeat for breakfast,
lunch and holiday meals.

Today Is

Sung to: "Mary Had a Little Lamb"

Today is _____,

_____, _____.

Today is _____,

Let's all sing a song.

It will be a fun day,

Fun day, fun day,

It will be a fun day,

All day long.

Let's sing about _____,

_____, _____.

Let's sing about _____,

All day long.

Fill in the blanks with the name of a
day. For example: Monday, Tuesday,
Katie's birthday, Valentine's Day, a
sunny day, a snowy day, a blue day,
a red day, etc.

The Bear Went Over the Mountain

The bear went over the mountain,
The bear went over the mountain,
The bear went over the mountain,
And what do you think he saw?

He saw a _____ _____,
He saw a _____ _____,
He saw a _____ _____.
And that is what he saw.

Let the children take turns naming things the bear
saw. For example: purple dragon, flying saucer,
big circus, candy store, etc.

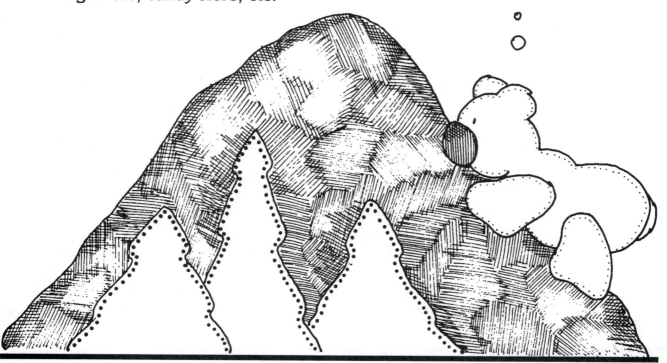

Have You Seen?

Sung to: "Did You Ever See a Lassie?"

Have you ever seen a _____,

A _____, a _____?

Have you ever seen a _____

That _____ _____ _____ _____?

That _____ and _____,

And _____ and _____?

Have you ever seen a _____

That _____ _____ _____ _____?

Have fun with this song. Fill in the blanks to sing
about anything you want. For example:

Have you ever seen a pumpkin,

A pumpkin, a pumpkin?

Have you ever seen a pumpkin

That grows big and round?

That grows and grows

And grows and grows.

Have you ever seen a pumpkin

That grows big and round?

Have you ever seen a girl,

A girl, a girl?

Have you ever seen a girl

Who jumps up and down?

Who jumps and jumps

And jumps and jumps.

Have you ever seen a girl

That jumps up and down?

Zoo Animals

Sung to: "Did You Ever See a Lassie?"

Have you ever seen the _____,

The _____, the _____?

Have you ever seen the _____

That lives in the zoo?

Have your children take turns naming zoo animals to sing about. Or let each child sing a verse by him or herself, naming whatever animal he or she wishes.

Time Song
Sung to: "London Bridge"

Now it's time to

_____ _____ _____,

_____ _____ _____,

_____ _____ _____.

Now it's time to

_____ _____ _____

For it is _____ o'clock.

Have your children sing about various activities and the times they are done. For example: Now it's time to go to school, for it is nine o'clock; Now it's time to eat our lunch, for it is twelve o'clock; Now it's time to go to bed, for it is eight o'clock; etc.

On Our Way to School

Sung to: "The Mulberry Bush"

Here we go _____ down the street,

Down the street, down the street.

Here we go _____ down the street

On our way to school.

Have your children name different ways they can
get to school. Sing a verse for each one and have
the children move in that way. For example:
marching, bouncing, jumping, rolling, etc.

What Do You Think of That?

Sung to: "For He's a Jolly Good Fellow"

Oh, we are _____ children,

Oh, we are _____ children,

Oh, we are _____ children,

Now what do you think of that?

Help the children think of words that describe them, such as happy, funny, smart, hungry, silly, etc. Then let the children choose which ones to sing about.

Feeling Song

Sung to: "If You're Happy and You Know It"

If you're _____ and you know it,

_____ _____ _____.

If you're _____ and you know it,

_____ _____ _____.

If you're _____ and you know it,

Then your face will surely show it.

If you're _____ and you know it,

_____ _____ _____.

Help your children think of feelings and ways to show them. Then have them sing about them in this song. For example:

If you're sad and you know it,

Cry boo-hoo.

If you're sad and you know it,

Cry boo-hoo.

If you're sad and you know it,

Then your face will surely show it.

If you're sad and you know it,

Cry boo-hoo.

Cleanup Song

Sung to: "The Paw Paw Patch"

Let's pick up the _____,

And put them in the _____.

Let's pick up the _____

And put them in the _____.

Let's pick up the _____

And put them in the _____

So our room will be all clean.

Have your children name things they can put away and where they put them. For example: Let's pick up the blocks and put them on the shelf; Let's pick up the dolls and put them in the corner; Let's pick up the coats and put them on the hooks, etc.

As You Turn Around

Sung to: "Row, Row, Row Your Boat"

_____, _____, _____ your _____,

_____ them up and down.

_____ like this and _____ like that

As you turn around.

Let your children name body parts and ways to move them. Then sing a song for each. For example:

Wiggle, wiggle, wiggle your toes,

Wiggle them up and down.

Wiggle like this and wiggle like that

As you turn around.

Grandma's Coming

Sung to: "She'll Be Coming Round the Mountain"

She'll be driving a _____ _____

When she comes.

She'll be driving a _____ _____

When she comes.

She'll be driving a _____ _____,

She'll be driving a _____ _____.

Oh, she'll be driving a _____ _____

When she comes.

Let your children name types of transportation that a grandparent or other special person could use to come visit them. For example: old jalopy, big truck, funny bike, golf cart, school bus, motor home, green van, etc.

Play With Me

Sung to: "Mary Had a Little Lamb"

_____ _____ by the tree,

By the tree, by the tree.

_____ _____ by the tree,

Won't you come and play with me?

Have your children sing about animals they would like to play with. For example: fluffy puppy, pretty kitty, shy little pony, cute little squirrel, great big elephant, little gray mouse, etc.

The Lost Song

Sung to: "Mary Had a Little Lamb"

Do you know where my _____ is,

My _____ is, my _____ is?

Do you know where my _____ is?

I lost my _____ today.

Have the children take turns naming things to
pretend they have lost. Then sing a verse for each
item. For example: pencil, mitten, hat, sweater,
dog, teddy bear, teacher, etc.

Special Times Song
Sung to: "The Farmer in the Dell"

_____ time is here.

_____ time is here.

Heigh-ho and away we go,

_____ time is here.

Have your children sing about special times of the day or year. For example: lunch, nap, bath, Christmas, summer, etc.

The Fly Song

Sung to: "The Farmer in the Dell"

A fly is on my _____,

A fly is on my _____.

Heigh-ho the derry-oh,

A fly is on my _____.

Have your children name parts of their bodies
that an imaginary fly might land on for them to
sing about.

Round and Round

Sung to: "The Wheels On the Bus"

Oh, the _____ on the _____

Go round and round,

Round and round,

Round and round.

Oh, the _____ on the _____

Go round and round

All day long.

Have your children fill in things that go round and round. For example: propellers on the plane, skaters in the rink, people on the rides, hands on the clock, etc.

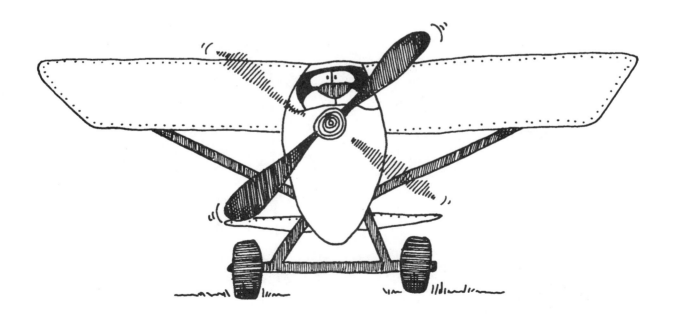

I Hear

Sung to: "Frere Jacques"

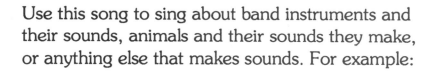

I hear _____ _____ ,
I hear _____ _____ .
Hear them _____ ,
Hear them _____ .

_____ _____ _____ ,
_____ _____ _____ .
Hear them _____ ,
Hear them _____ .

Use this song to sing about band instruments and
their sounds, animals and their sounds they make,
or anything else that makes sounds. For example:

I hear drums beat,

I hear drums beat.

Hear them beat,

Hear them beat.

Rat-a-tat-a-tat-tat,

Rat-a-tat-a-tat-tat.

Hear them beat,

Hear them beat.

I hear dogs bark,

I hear dogs bark.

Hear them bark,

Hear them bark.

Arf-arf-arf-arf-arf-arf,

Arf-arf-arf-arf-arf-arf.

Hear them bark,

Hear them bark.

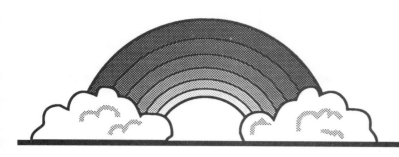

The Zoo

I love the zoo.

There are so many animals to see.

The silliest animal is the _____.

The tallest animal is the _____.

The smallest animal is the _____.

The friendliest animal is the _____.

The fattest animal is the _____.

The noisiest animal is the _____.

The cleanest animal is the _____.

The prettiest animal is the _____.

My favorite animal is the _____.

If I had room, I would keep a _____ in my yard.

My Sandwich

I'm making myself a sandwich.

First I take out two pieces of _____.

Next I spread on some _____.

Then I add a _____.

Next come two pieces of _____.

Then I add some _____ and a sprinkle of _____.

Mmmm, it looks so good!

I put everything on top of each other and top it off with _____.

I like to make my own sandwich.

The Merry-Go-Round

I love to ride on the merry-go-round.

It spins around like a _____.

The cheerful music makes me want to _____.

When I ride around, I feel like a _____.

My favorite horse is painted _____.

I love to ride on the merry-go-round.

If I had my own merry-go-round, I would keep it _____.

A Rainbow

I see a rainbow.

It is more colorful than _____.

My favorite rainbow color is _____.

If I look under the rainbow, I will find _____.

To catch a rainbow, I will _____.

I can use my rainbow to _____.

If I had two rainbows, I would give one to _____.

Colors

The world is full of colors.

The coldest color I can think of is _____.

The warmest color I can think of is _____.

The softest color I can think of is _____.

The scariest color I can think of is _____.

When I think of yellow, I think of _____.

When I think of red, I think of _____.

When I think of blue, I think of _____.

When I think of green, I think of _____.

My favorite color for a house is _____.

My favorite color for a flower is _____.

The funniest color I can think of is _____.

The color that makes me the happiest is _____.

Snow

Snowflakes fall as softly as _____ and as quietly

as _____.

The snow is as cold as _____.

I love to watch the snow cover up _____.

I love walking in the snow like a _____.

I think I will save some snow in my _____.

The snow makes me happy because _____.

Sometimes the snow makes me sad because _____.

My Snow Pal

I have fun when it snows.

I can make a Snow Pal as round as a _____.

I can make a face for my Snow Pal with _____.

I can make arms for my Snow Pal with _____.

I know my Snow Pal is happy because _____.

I am going to name my Snow Pal _____.

My Snow Pal is my friend.

Clouds

I watched the clouds today.

A great big cloud reminded me of a _____.

Another one made me hungry because it looked like _____.

Another one was round like a _____.

Next to it was a cloud that looked like a stuffed _____.

The cloud I liked best looked like _____.

I like looking at the clouds.

The Beach

I went to the beach today.

The sun was as hot as _____.

The sky was as blue as _____.

The water was as cold as _____.

I swam in the water just like a _____.

I played in the sand and built a _____.

While I was digging in the sand, I found a _____.

I love to run on the beach like a _____.

I had fun at the beach.

Surprises

Sometimes surprises are round like _____.

Sometimes surprises are wrapped up like _____.

Sometimes surprises are loud like _____.

Sometimes surprises are small like _____.

Sometimes surprises are cold like _____.

Sometimes surprises are funny like _____.

I like surprises!

Happy Birthday

Today is my birthday.

I feel as old as _____.

I am happy because _____.

I think I will wear my _____ today.

My cake looks like a _____.

I hope we have ice cream that tastes like _____.

What I really want for my birthday is _____.

I opened a small present. It was a _____.

Birthdays make me feel _____.

I wish it was my birthday every day!

Toys

I am shopping for a toy.

The biggest toy I see is a _____.

The funniest toy I see is a _____.

Some toys can move; the one I like best is a _____.

The smallest round toy I see is a _____.

The softest toy I see is a _____.

Some toys you play with outside; the one I like best is a _____.

Some toys you can take to bed with you; the one I like best

    is a _____.

Some toys you can play with by yourself; the one I like best

    is a _____.

Some toys you need other people to play with; the one I like

    best is a _____.

The toy I would most like to buy is a _____.

The Christmas Tree

I love to sit and look at our Christmas tree.

It makes me happy because _____.

My favorite ornament is _____.

The lights sparkle like _____.

The bulbs are shaped like _____.

At the top we put a _____.

I like to help put on the _____.

When I see the tree all lit up, it makes me

     want to _____.

I love looking at our Christmas tree.

Homemade Cookies

I love to help make cookies.

Sometimes the dough smells like _____.

When I roll out the dough it looks like a great big _____.

My favorite cookie cutter is the _____.

The smallest cookie I ever made looked like a _____.

After we bake cookies, sometimes we frost them.

My favorite flavor of frosting is _____.

The funniest cookie I ever made was a _____.

Making cookies is fun, but eating them is even more fun.

Farm Animals

One day I went to visit a farm.

There were animals everywhere.

The biggest animal I saw was a _____.

The oldest animal I saw was a _____.

The youngest animal I saw was a _____.

The noisiest animals were the _____.

The softest animals were the _____.

The friendliest animal was a _____.

I went for a ride on a _____.

If I could choose one of the animals to take home,

I would choose the _____.

Playdough

I like to make things out of playdough.

First I roll the dough into a big mound like a _____.

Then I roll it into a long rope that looks like a _____.

Next I do some baking with my playdough.

I make some _____ and some _____.

The smallest thing I ever made was a _____.

The funniest thing I ever made was a _____.

Sometimes I use a knife with my playdough and cut out _____.

Sometimes I use a rolling pin and make _____.

My favorite color for playdough is _____.

My very favorite thing to make out of playdough is _____.

Box Rides

One day I found a big box.

I climbed aboard and pretended to go for a ride.

First I went for a super fast ride in a _____.

Next I flew way up high in a _____.

Then I was carried across the sea in a _____.

The scariest ride was in a _____.

The slowest ride was in a _____.

The coldest ride was in a _____.

My favorite ride was in a _____.

Big boxes give great rides!

Symbol Stories

Symbol stories encourage children to use their imagination. Set up a story line, using symbols such as circles, squares and wavy lines. Let a child assign a word to each symbol. Additional words can be used between symbols to connect the story ideas. Start with simple one-line stories, then gradually write longer ones.

For example: One child may "read" the symbol story above like this, "The mother bear and the baby bear ran down to the lake. They caught three fish and took them home." Another child may read the story like this, "The truck and the little car drove over the mountain and stopped at a big town. They stayed three days and then went home."

What kind of stories can the children tell using the symbols below?

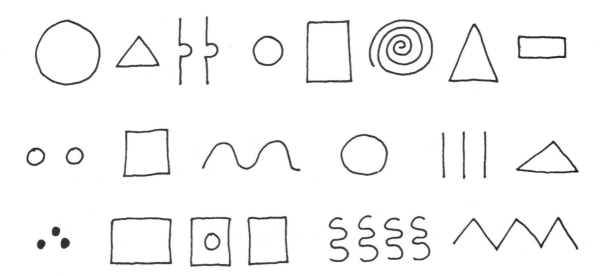

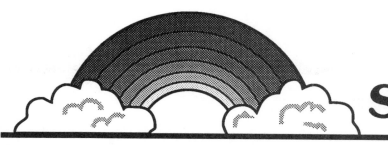

SOLUTIONS

Baby Bird

A bird fell out of its nest. How will the baby get back in the nest?

Possible Solutions:

The baby could learn to fly and fly back up.

The wind could blow the baby bird back up.

The mother or father bird could carry it back up.

The mother or father could bring the nest down to the baby bird.

They could rent a crane.

They could teach the baby bird how to climb a ladder.

The Picnic

The children have come to the park for a picnic.
When they unpack their lunch, they find out that
their juice is in a large bottle and they have
forgotten to bring their cups. How can they drink
the juice that is in the bottle?

Possible Solutions:

Go home and get their cups.

Make cups out of paper plates.

Wait to drink the juice until they get home.

Use their hands as cups.

Stick straws into the bottle.

Go to the store and buy cups.

Here to There

Name a place that is nearby or in the same building where you are, such as the sandbox. Ask your children to think of different ways to get from where they are to that other place.

Possible Solutions:

Go down the hall and out the back door.

Go through the window and around the house.

Go out the front door, around the block and then back through the yard.

You can also play this type of game with your children using a large map board. Have two or three children start at one point and ask them to find different routes to the same destination.

Wonder Why

Take advantage of any unusual situation that you and your children observe. If you see a family traveling in a car with a bird cage tied to the roof, encourage your children to make up reasons why.

Possible Solutions:

They have lost their pet bird and are trying to catch a new one.

They are letting the wind clean out the cage.

They are using the cage for a radio antenna.

Their car is crowded and they could not fit it inside.

The cage smelled too much to carry in the car.

They are going through a car wash, and they want to wash the cage at the same time.

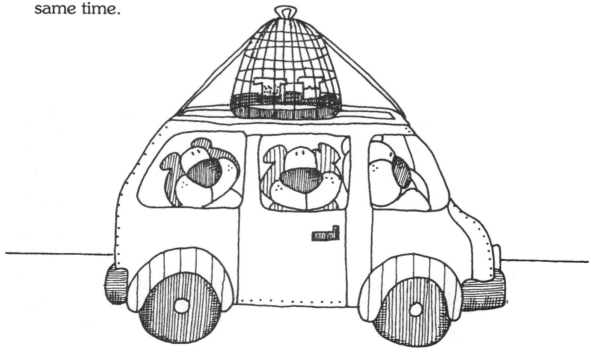

Giant Pumpkin

Tell your children a tale about two children who have grown a beautiful big pumpkin. The trouble is that the pumpkin grew too big for them to carry. The children want to take it to the fair and enter it in a pumpkin contest, but they can't move it. What can they do?

Possible Solutions:

Rent a crane.

Get their parents to help them lift the pumpkin.

Roll it to the fair.

Carve out the middle of the pumpkin to make it lighter.

Send a picture of it to the fair.

Roll it onto a blanket and pull it to the fair.

My Friend's Birthday

It is your friend's birthday and you do not have any money. What can you give your friend for a present?

Possible Solutions:

A hug and a kiss.

A picture you've made.

A toy you don't want any more.

Some wild flowers you've picked.

Some cookies you've baked.

Adapt this activity to a parent's or a sibling's birthday if it is appropriate.

Ice Cream Store

Pretend that you are opening up a new ice cream store. Ask your children to help you invent some new flavors. Let the children take turns naming new flavors.

Possible Solutions:

Pizza ice cream.

Cherry-banana ice cream.

Rainbow ice cream.

Hot dog ice cream.

What's the Question?

Play this game with your children. Give them an
"answer" and have them think of a question that
fits it.

Examples:

If the answer is "Red," the question could be "What color is my shirt?"

If the answer is "Five," the question could be "How old am I?"

If the answer is "Round," the question could be "What shape is a ball?"

You may need to give the children many examples
before they understand how the game is played.
You can also begin by playing the game in reverse,
and have the children give the "answer" while you
make up a question.

Donut Holes

Generate a discussion with your children about
why donuts have holes.

Possible Solutions:

They cook faster that way.

They are easier to eat.

You can stack them all on a long stick.

You can carry one on your finger.

You can string them like beads.

When they get hard, you can use them for a ring toss game.

Christmas Tree Mystery

One day Mrs. Jones came home and found her Christmas tree lying on the ground. What could have happened?

Possible Solutions:

A cat jumped on the tree while chasing a bird.

The baby pulled on an ornament and tipped the tree over.

Someone opened a window and the wind blew it over.

A dog chased a cat up the tree.

Santa Claus tripped over a toy and fell on it.

Tree Decorations

Not too long ago, families decorated their Christmas trees with only handmade ornaments. Ask your children to imagine a time when there were no Christmas lights or other ready-made ornaments. How could they decorate their tree?

Possible Solutions:

String popcorn or cranberries to hang on the tree.

Make paper ornaments.

Hang small toys on the tree.

Pick flowers and put them on the tree.

Light small candles in holders on the tree.

Hang sparkling jewels on the tree.

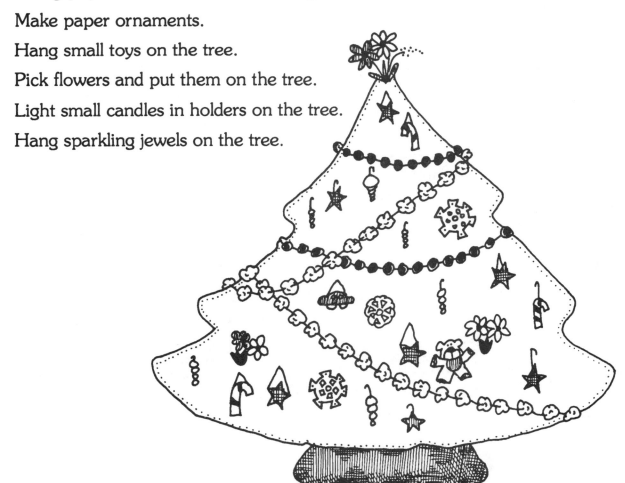

Easter Bunny Problems

It's Eastertime and the Easter Bunny has run out of egg dye. How else can he color his eggs?

Possible Solutions:

Color them with crayons.

Color them with felt-tip markers.

Wrap them with colored yarn.

Dip them in beet juice.

Paint them.

Paste sequins on them.

Cover them with glue and sprinkle on glitter.

The Easter Bunny has run out of eggs. What else can he put in his baskets?

Possible Solutions:

Small toys.

Paper eggs.

Cookies shaped like bunnies and eggs.

Fruit.

Tennis balls.

The Easter Bunny has run out of artificial grass for his Easter baskets. What else can he use?

Possible Solutions:

Shredded newspapers.

Cut-up green tissue paper.

Real grass.

Leaves.

Cotton balls.

Plastic foam packing peanuts.

The Easter Bunny has broken his leg and can't hop very fast. How can he deliver all of his baskets?

Possible Solutions:

Hire an airplane and drop the baskets with parachutes.

Ride on a skateboard.

Learn how to fly by flapping his ears.

Send them in the mail.

How Many Ways?

How many ways can you get across the room?

How many ways can you say "Happy Birthday?"

How many ways can you keep cool in the summertime?

How many ways can you cook an egg?

How many ways can you go downstairs?

How many ways can you pop a balloon?

How many ways can you eat peanut butter?

How many ways can you show you are angry?

How many ways can you show you are happy?

How many ways can you get across a river?

How many ways can Santa get down a chimney?

How many ways can you catch a monster?

How many ways can you catch a fish?

How many ways can you play with a ball?

How many ways can you say "Thank you?"

Would You Rather?

Would you rather be an elephant or a mouse?

Would you rather be a mother or a father?

Would you rather be a raindrop or a snowflake?

Would you rather be Little Red Riding Hood or Goldilocks?

Would you rather be a farm animal or a fish?

Would you rather be hot or cold?

Would you rather work or play?

Would you rather eat spinach or liver?

Would you rather sing or dance?

Would you rather ride on a train or a plane?

Would you rather watch a movie or a play?

Would you rather eat ice cream or cake?

Would you rather it was Christmas or Hanukkah or your birthday?

Would you rather live in an igloo or a tepee?

What If?

What if you had your own robot?

What if you broke your friend's favorite toy?

What if your teddy bear could sing and dance?

What if it rained all the time?

What if everything around you was the same color?

What if there were no cars?

What if animals could talk?

What if everyone looked the same?

What if you were no bigger than your thumb?

What if you lived in a house made of ice?

What if money grew on trees?

What if the world was totally covered with water?

What if people could not talk?

What if you could fly?

What if it never got dark?

Active preschool learning— Ideas that work!

From Totline® Publications

Totline® MAGAZINE

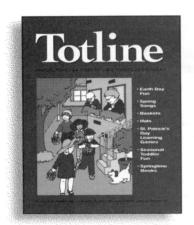

Now in full color!

Challenge and engage young children with the fresh ideas for active learning in *Totline Magazine*. Developed with busy, early-childhood professionals and parents in mind, these activities need minimal preparation for successful learning fun. Each bimonthly issue is perfect for working with children ages two to six and includes • seasonal learning themes • stories, songs, and rhymes • open-ended art projects and science explorations • reproducible parent pages • ready-made teaching materials • and activites just for toddlers. *Totline Magazine* is the perfect resource for a project-based curriculum in a preschool or at home.

Reproducible! Super Snack News

This delicious newsletter is meant to be shared!

Make up to 200 copies per issue with each subscription, then use the copies as informative handouts! *Super Snack News* is a monthly, four-page newsletter featuring healthy recipes that parents and preschoolers will love, learning activities perfect for the home environment, plus nutrition tips. Also provided are category guidelines for the Child and Adult Care Food Program (CACFP). Sharing *Super Snack News* is a wonderful way to help promote parent involvement in quality childcare.